# The Elves and the Shoemaker

by Mike Brownlow

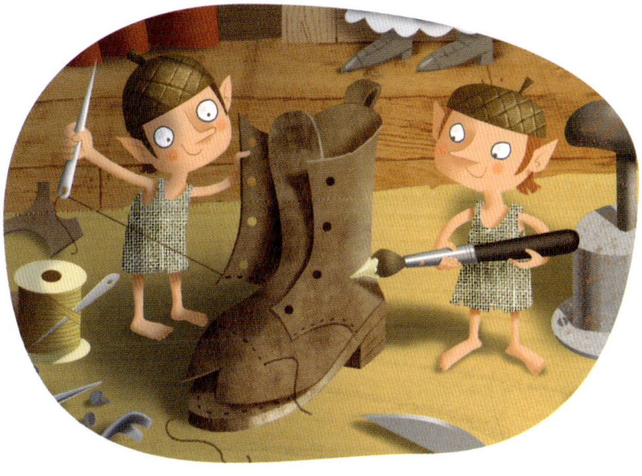

OXFORD
UNIVERSITY PRESS

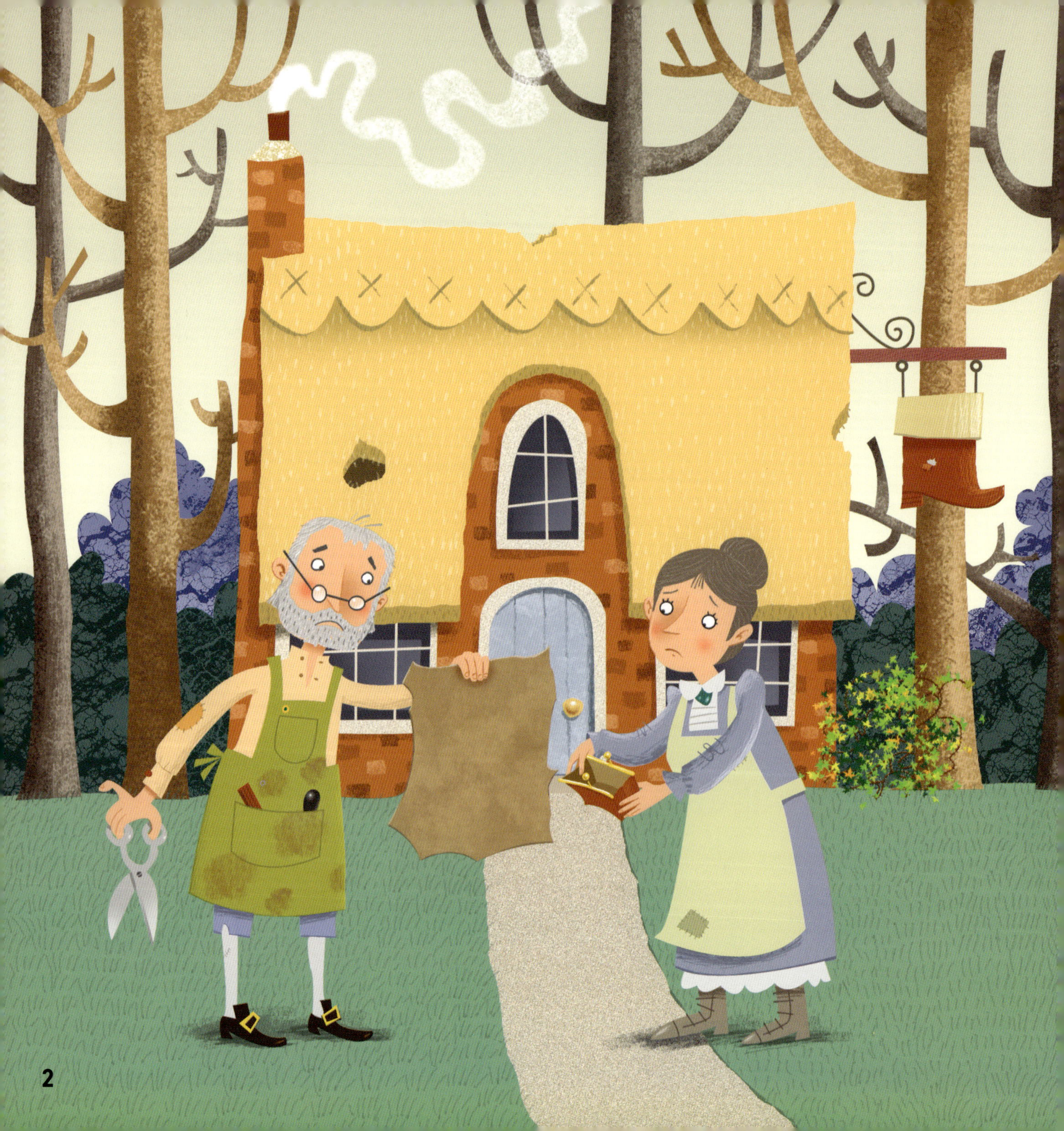

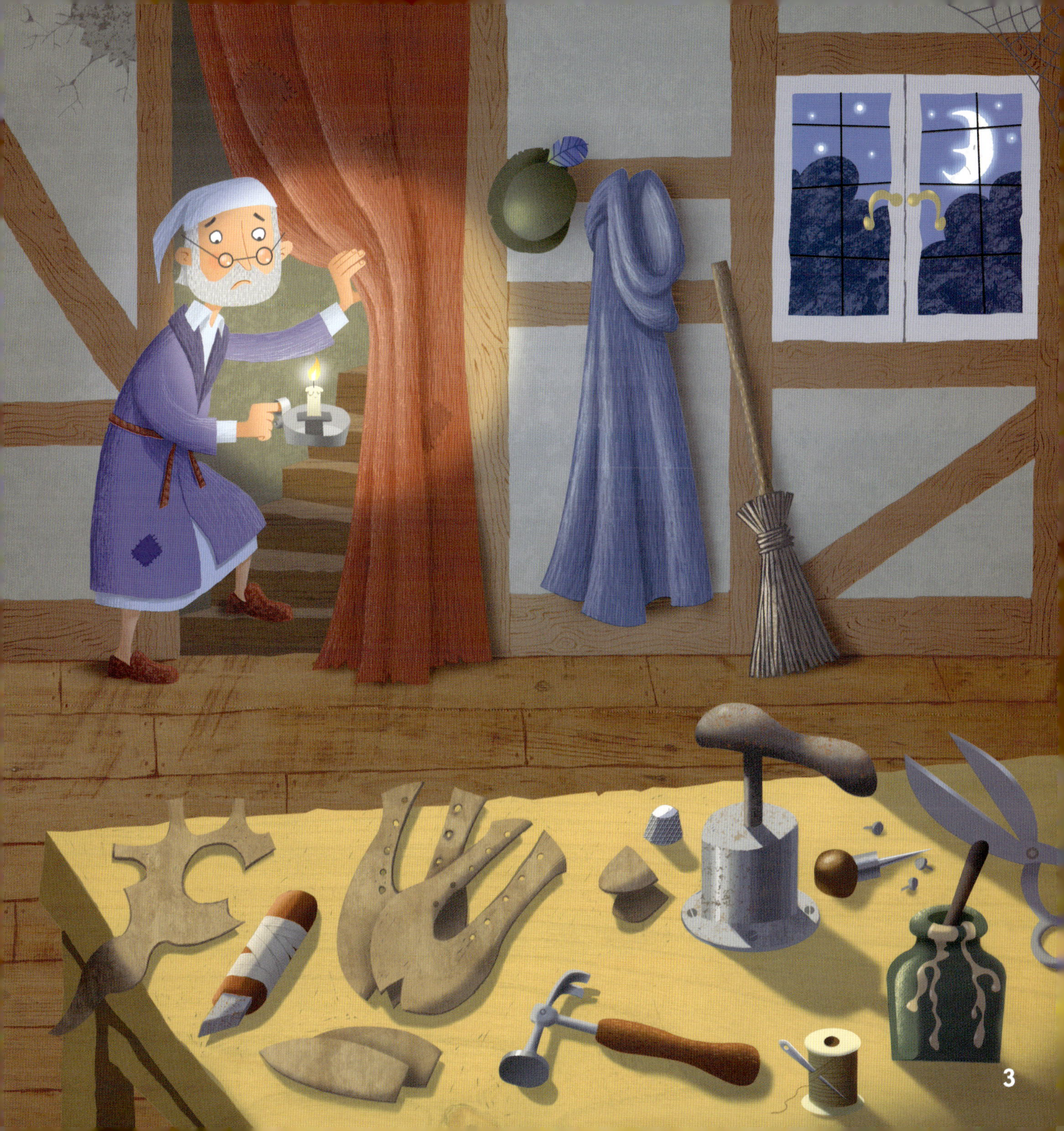

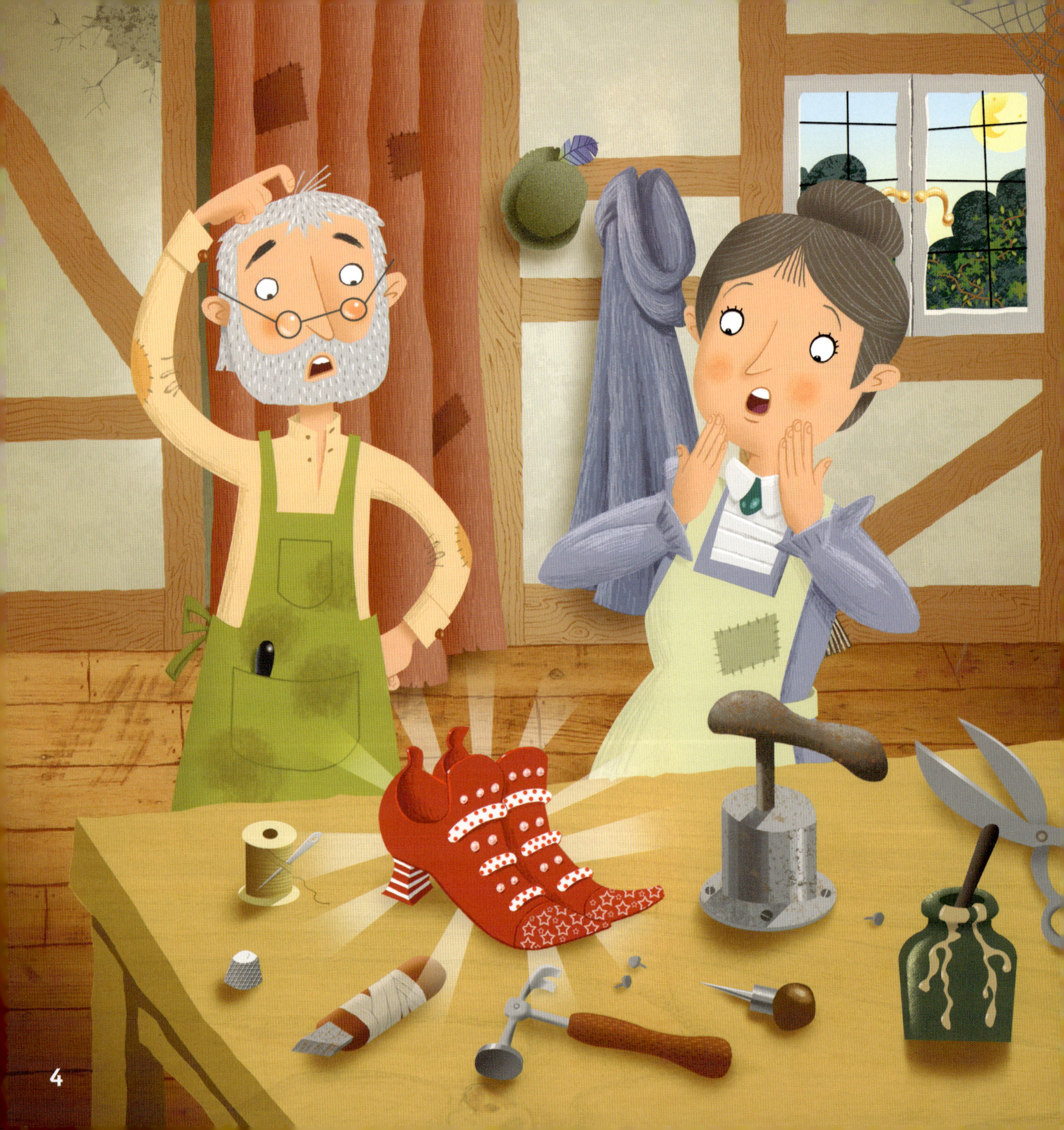

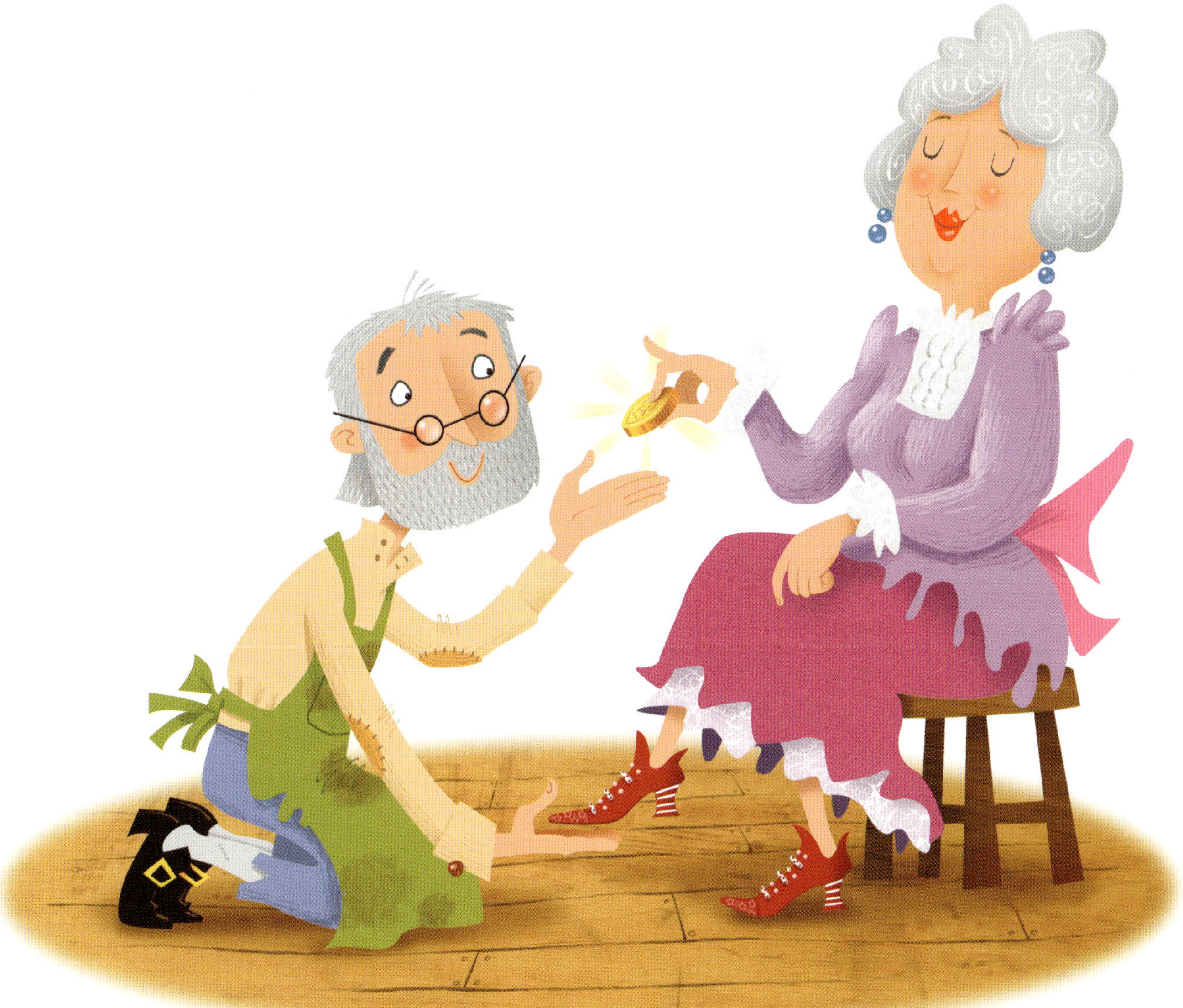

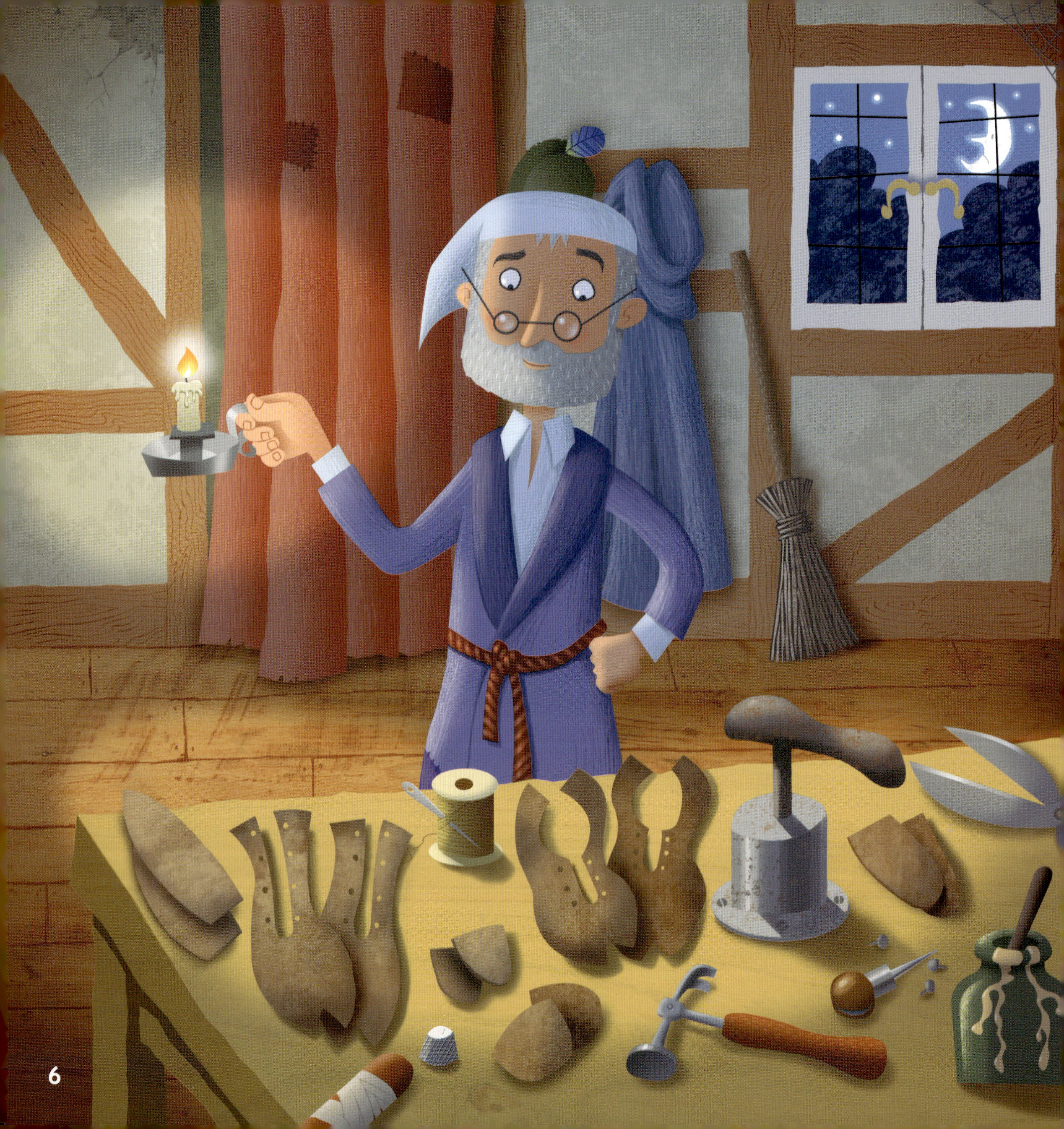

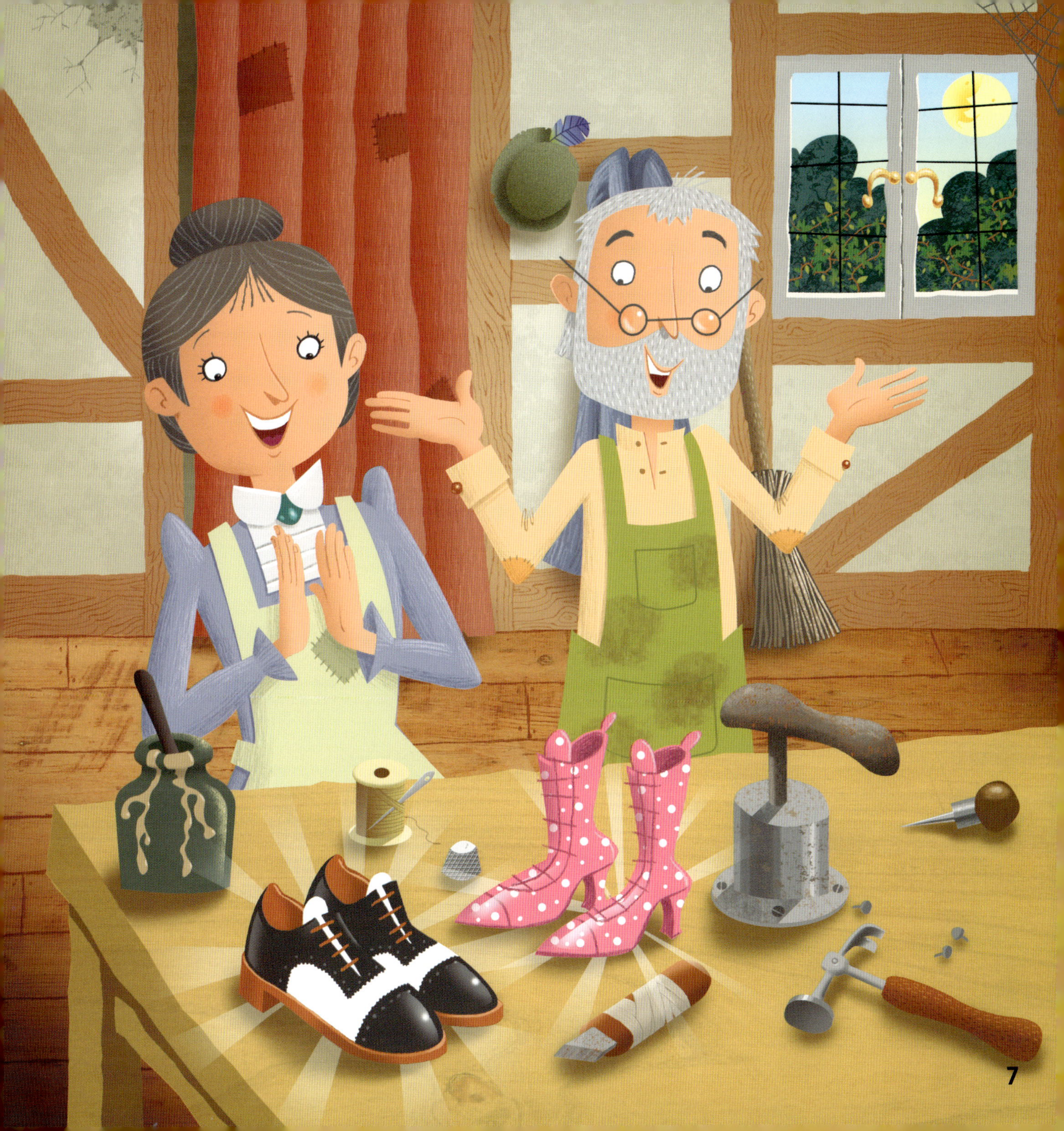

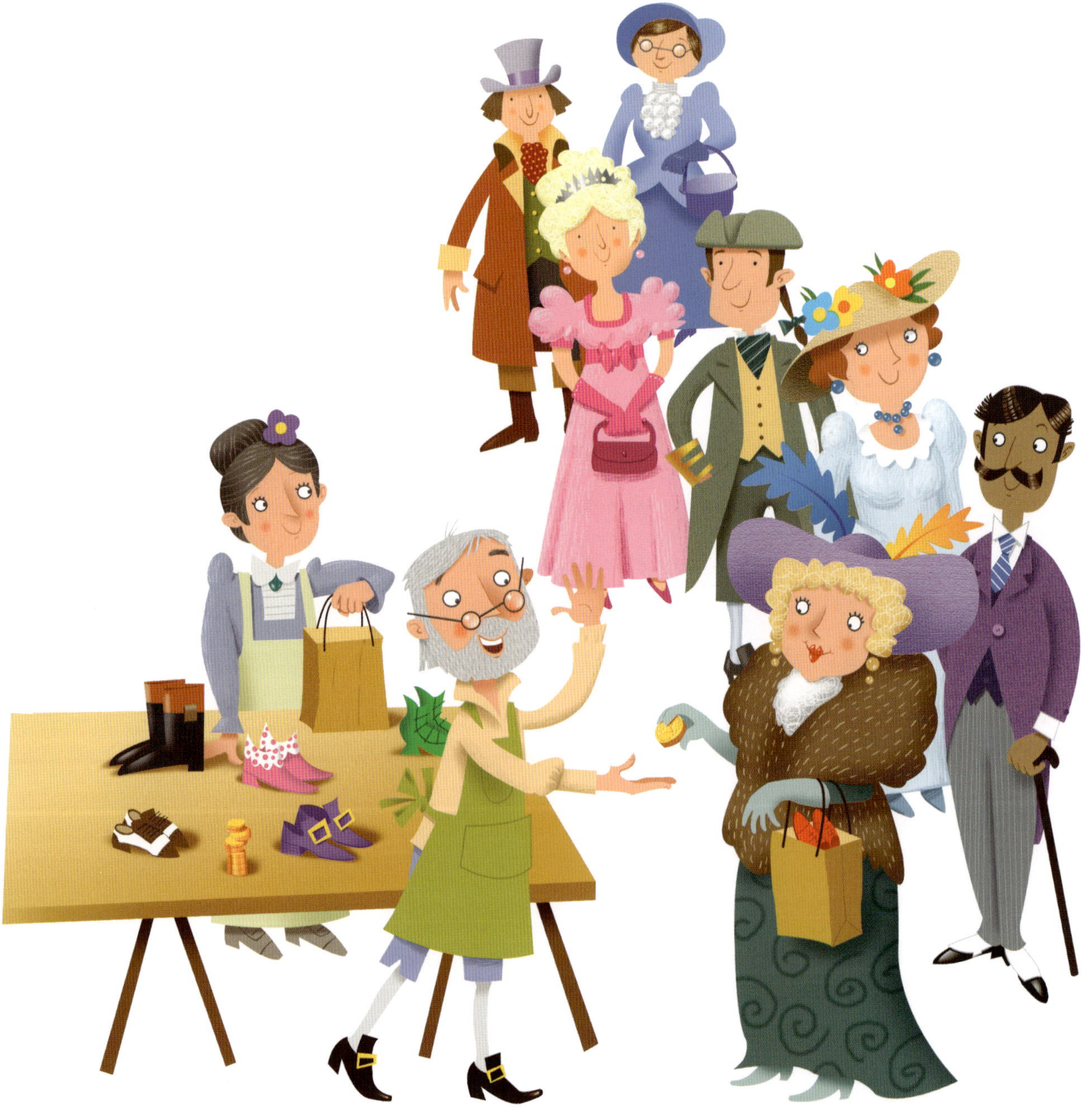

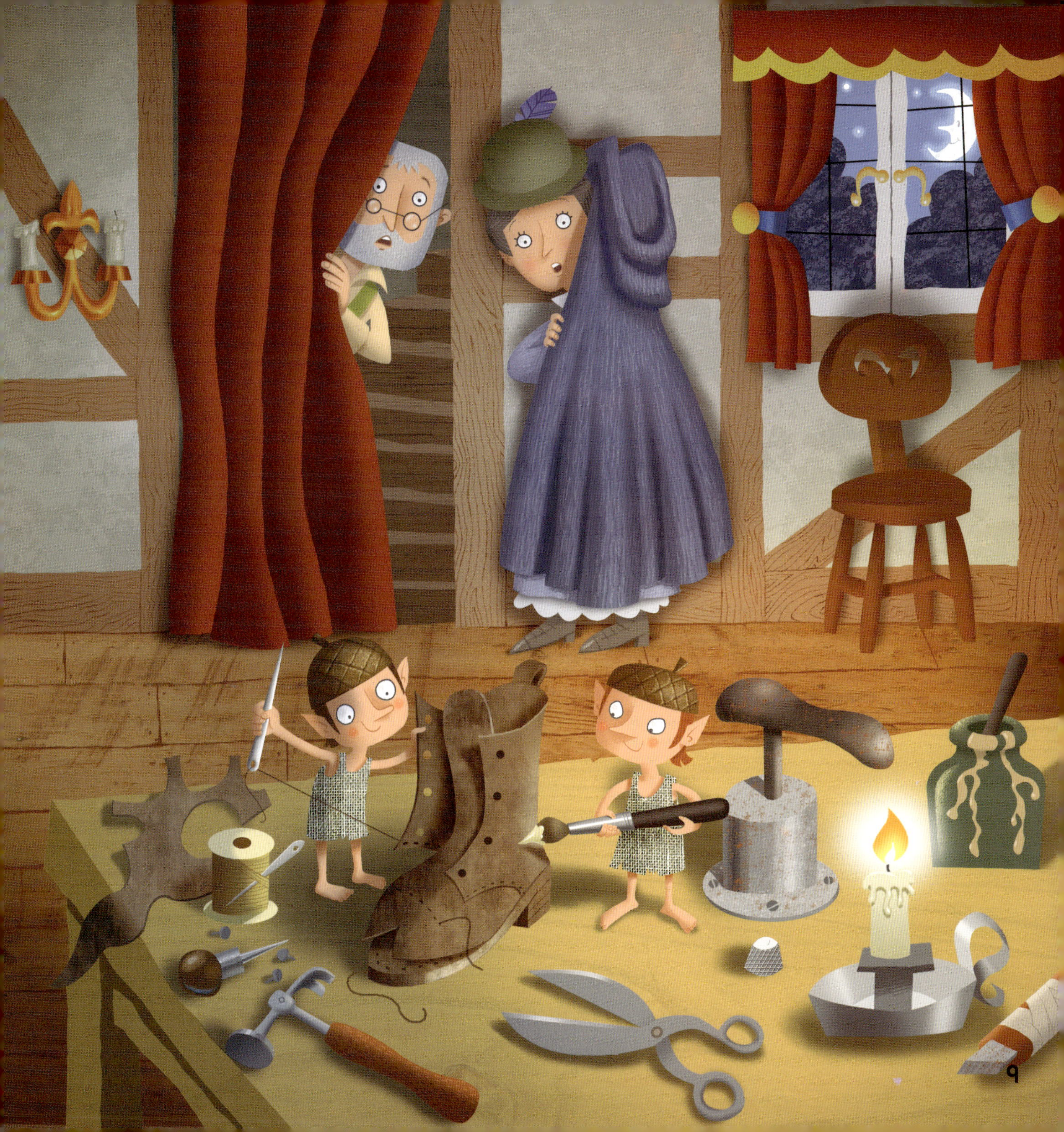

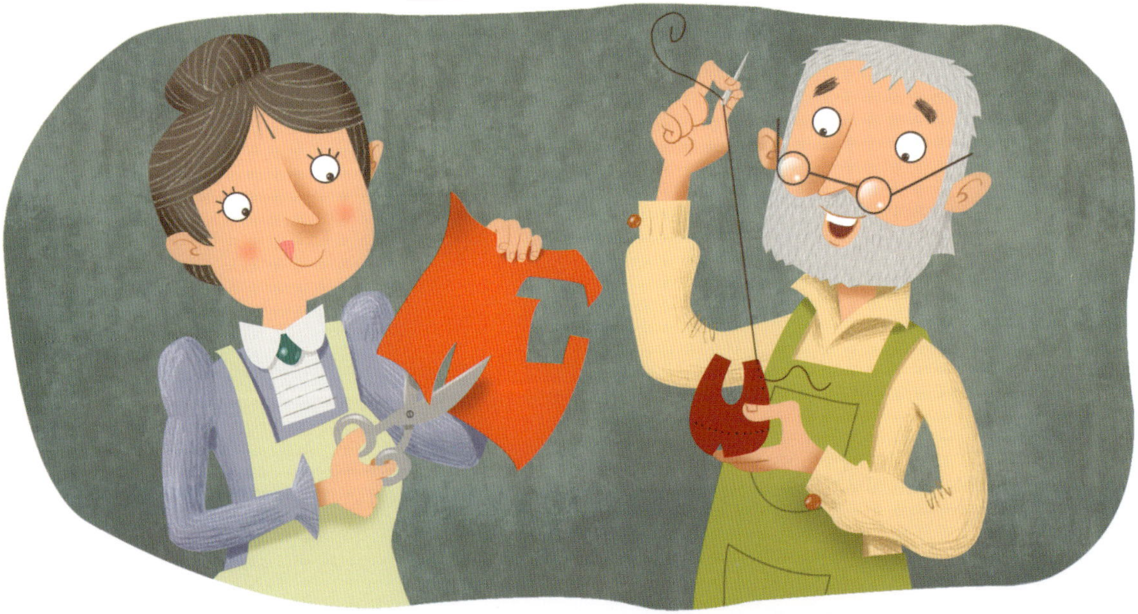

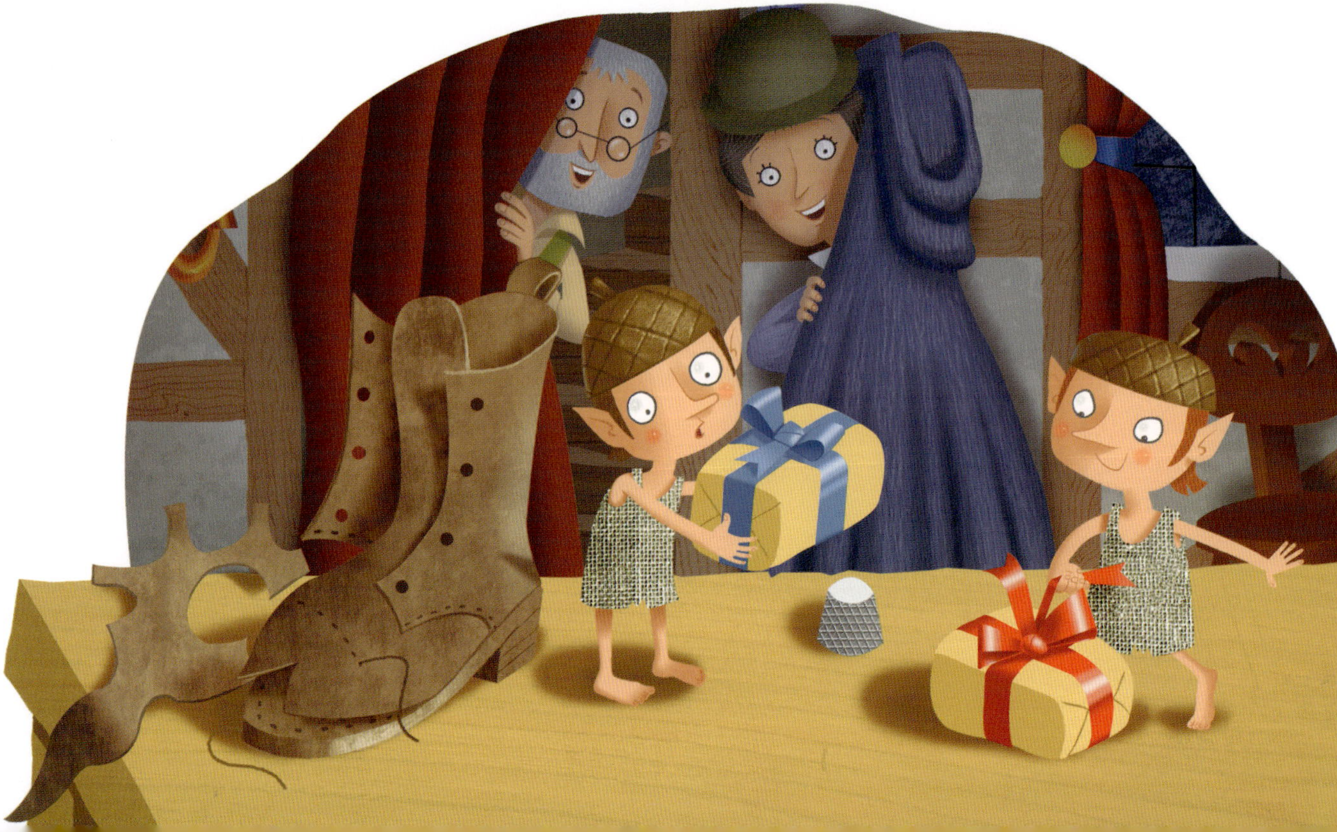

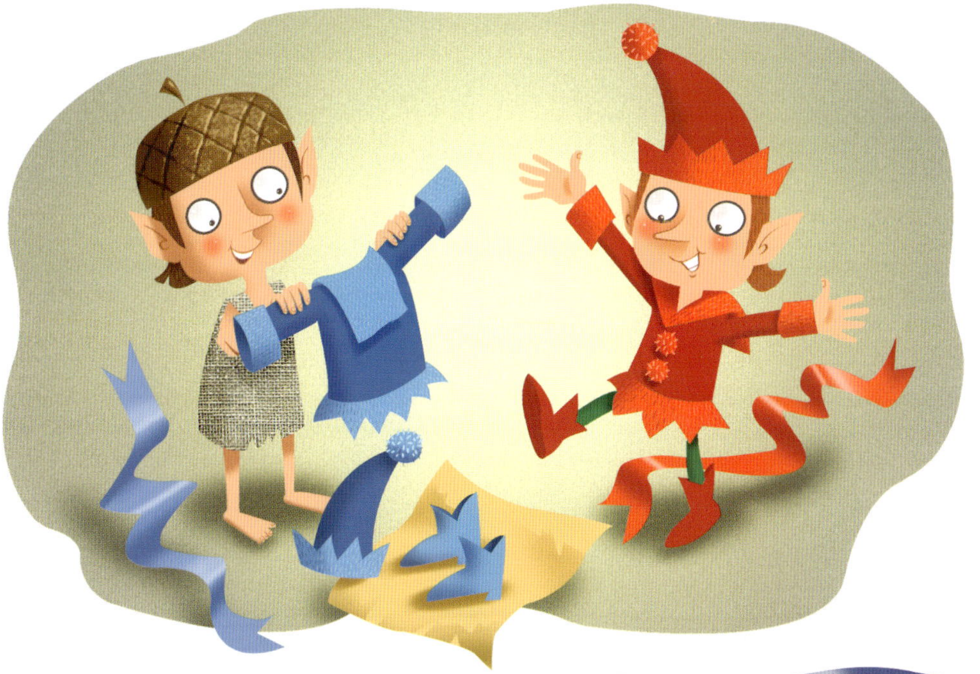

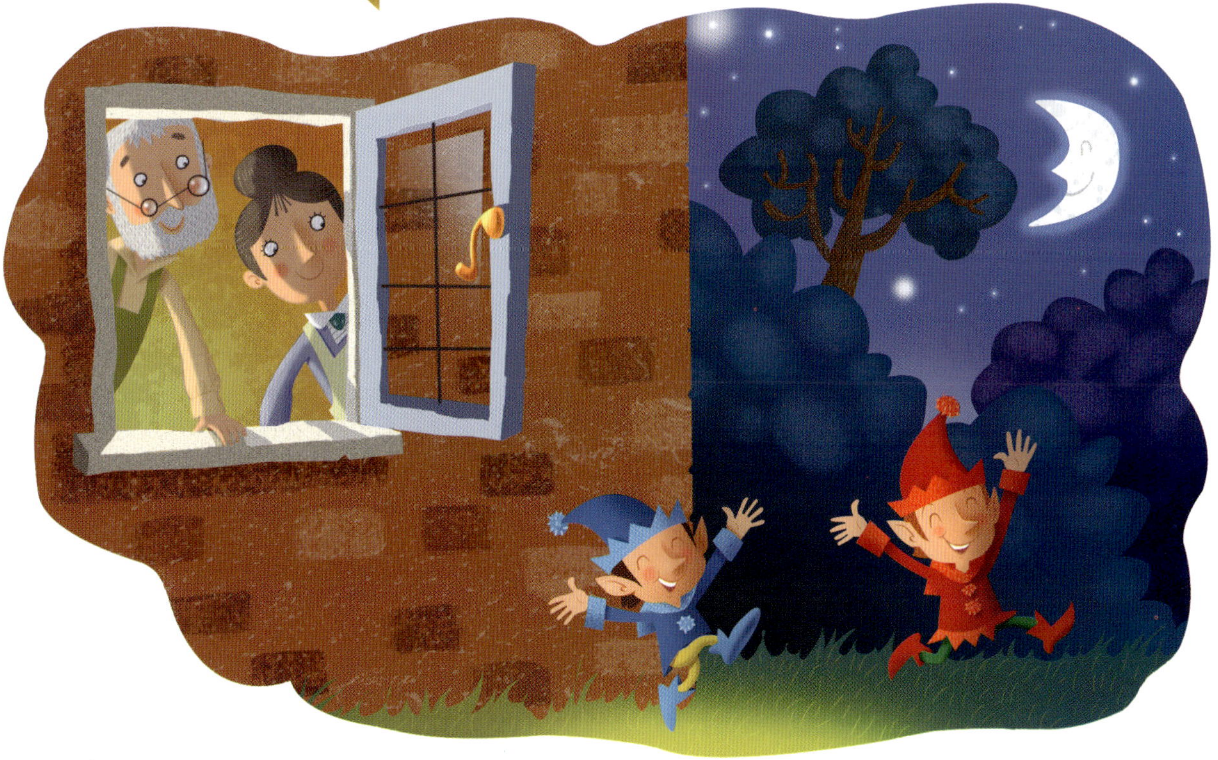

## Retell the story

**Once upon a time...**

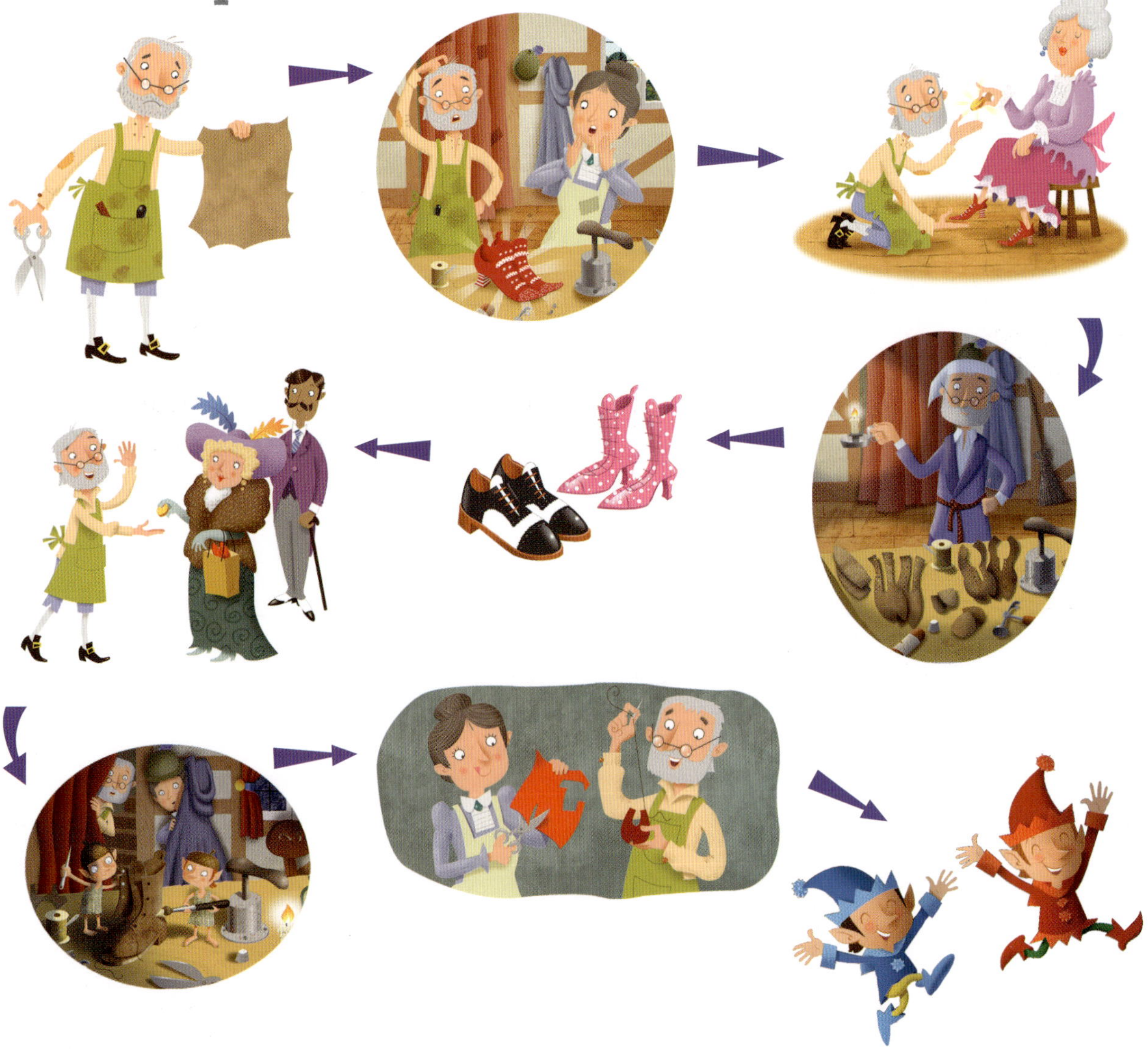

**The end.**